CHRISTIANS-IN-THE-MAKING
ROD SARGENT

NAVPRESS

A MINISTRY OF THE NAVIGATORS
P.O. Box 6000, Colorado Springs, CO 80934

Photography by Bill Bruin

The Navigators is an international, evangelical
Christian organization. Jesus Christ gave his
followers the Great Commission to go and make
disciples (Matthew 28:19). The aim of The Navigators
is to help fulfill that commission by multiplying
laborers for Christ in every nation.

NavPress is the publishing ministry of The
Navigators. NavPress publications are tools to
help Christians grow. Although publications alone cannot
make disciples or change lives, they can help believers
learn biblical discipleship, and apply what they learn
to their lives and ministries.

Second printing, 1981

Printed in the United States of America

"I shall sing my song
of the pilgrimage I am making
from what I was to what God is making of me.
I say 'what God is making of me,'
for the best I can say about myself is that
I'm a Christian-in-the-making."

E. STANLEY JONES

Jones, E. Stanley. *A Song of Ascents.* (Nashville, Tennessee: Abingdon Press 1968, Festival edition 1979) page 17. Used by permission.

The life of the Christian-in-the-making begins with spiritual rebirth. As the new Christian begins growing, he shares the gospel with others; thus multiplying himself. The raw material in this process is a man who seeks God.

Oswald Chambers says the gospel is primarily creative, not persuasive. This means that we Christians need not go through the mental gymnastics of arguing with non-Christians as to why the gospel is believable. Nor should we feel triumphant or deflated, depending on who won the argument.

Peter wrote that we are "born again, not of corruptible seed, but of incorruptible, by the word of God, which liveth and abideth for ever" (1 Peter 1:23).

There is nothing persuasive about a seed. It has no arguments for being and has no offensive attack against the elements around it. When planted, it simply begins to grow . . . life springs from within it. A seed is primarily creative.

Our job as Christians is not answering controversial questions or making clever presentations about the Christian faith. This will not create life any more than planting marbles will produce a crop. Our job is seed-sowing. This work unleashes the power of life as the Spirit of God uses the seeds we sow. We need confidence that there is power in the word to *create*.

If we have this firmly in mind, then liberty and joy will characterize our witness for Christ. Such witnessing will never become merely discharging an obligation. God gives us the privilege of joining in his creative work!

God has a plan for the journey of each Christian, as every shipbuilder has a blueprint for building a ship.

"You saw me before I was born and scheduled each day of my life before I began to breathe. Every day was recorded in your Book!" (Psalm 139:16 LB).

Commenting on this passage, A.F. Kirkpatrick says, "Each day of his life was predetermined by the Creator and recorded in His Book, before one of them was in existence. This is a clear expression of the truth that there is an *ideal plan* of life providentially marked out for every individual."

Knowing God has a day-by-day plan for our lives should have a very comforting effect upon us continuously.

Yet we often get uptight over circumstances when they go against our wishes. We become anxious . . . irritated . . . distraught. We take life into our own hands and try to manipulate events. Our trust in the sovereignty of God flies out of the window, and we no longer live like people who believe that our God controls *each* day of our lives.

"We are born afresh in Christ, and born to do those good deeds which God planned for us to do" (Ephesians 2:10 PH).

Trust in God is the Christian's plumb line. The growing disciple cannot make it on his own, and no shipbuilder would construct his ship by "eye."

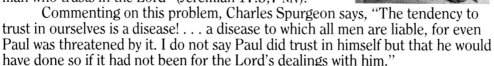

Does the question "Who can you trust these days?" cross your mind as often as it does mine?

Can you even trust yourself? This is equally important to ponder. Can you trust yourself to always do your absolute best? To never offend? To never neglect a duty? To always make totally objective decisions?

Of course not! Jeremiah warns us against self-trust: "Cursed is the one who trusts in man, . . . blessed is the man who trusts in the Lord" (Jeremiah 17:5,7 NIV).

Commenting on this problem, Charles Spurgeon says, "The tendency to trust in ourselves is a disease! . . . a disease to which all men are liable, for even Paul was threatened by it. I do not say Paul did trust in himself but that he would have done so if it had not been for the Lord's dealings with him."

Spurgeon continues, "The Lord warded off this evil by sending Paul a great trouble, and perhaps our heavenly Father is afflicting some of you in circumstances that are bewildering, all for this reason that you may become sick of yourself and fond of Christ . . . *Nothing can happen to you that is much worse than to trust yourself.*"

"Trust in the Lord with all thine heart; and lean not unto thine own understanding. In all thy ways acknowledge him, and he shall direct thy paths" (Proverbs 3:5-6).

A ship's frame is only as strong as its weakest point. Fortunately, the Christian is stronger than his weakest characteristic because Christ lives within him.

Have you ever thought about the balance needed between self-sufficiency and a dependent spirit?

Most of us have a propensity for being self-sufficient. This desire is inherent in our nature. When we meet our own needs successfully, we feel satisfied, proud, and comfortable . . . and that's a great feeling.

But is it possible that while zealously pursuing self-sufficiency we could fall into the trap of losing our lives while seemingly saving them?

The popular emphasis on developing self-confidence could easily obscure the *equally important* concept of the humble dependent spirit advocated in Scripture.

We cannot experience the absolute sufficiency of Christ as long as we insist on being totally self-sufficient.

Faith itself is a confession of personal inadequacy. Realizing we cannot save ourselves, we turn to our Savior.

Paul's words to the Corinthians reflect a strong sense of his own feelings of inadequacy. "I was with you in weakness, and in fear, and in much trembling" (1 Corinthians 2:3). Later he wrote, "I have cheerfully made up my mind to be proud of my weaknesses, because they mean a deeper experience of the power of Christ" (2 Corinthians 12:9 PH).

Jesus encouraged Paul by reminding him, "My grace is sufficient for you for my strength is made perfect in weakness." This truth can become real in your life as it was in Paul's.

Quality tools—an essential. We are God's instruments. We must heed our condition!

Holiness is not a list of universally approved dos and don'ts. Rather it is separation to God, and from the ungodly, the ordinary, and the common. Our greatest danger as Christians usually lies not in profane acts, but in allowing common, daily activities to crowd Christ out of our lives.

Our sophisticated age places great emphasis on the appearance of the outer man. Take hair, for instance. We cut, set, comb, and brush it. We also dress the outer man in the latest fashions. He requires constant, daily care—yet his deterioration is fantastically rapid! In less than twenty-four hours he is a mess if he is not maintained.

But how about the inner man? From his scriptural description, and personal observation, he is a most disreputable character! All of man's thoughts are evil continually, according to Genesis 6:5. But the Christian's standard for the inner man is, "As the One who called you is holy, so you yourselves should be holy in all your conduct" (1 Peter 1:15 BERK).

Philosophers tell us to abandon wickedness through self-effort . . . to substitute moderation and temperance for excess. The apostle Paul presents Christ as our deliverer. Strength comes when we "put on the Lord Jesus Christ, and make no provision for the flesh, to gratify its desires" (Romans 13:14 RSV).

A penetrating observation made years ago by Robert Murray McCheyne is a good reminder today: "How diligently the cavalry officer keeps his sabre clean. Every stain is wiped off with the greatest of care. We are His instruments. In great measure, according to the purity and perfection of the instrument, will be the fruitfulness." Holiness involves keeping clean and pure so God can use us.

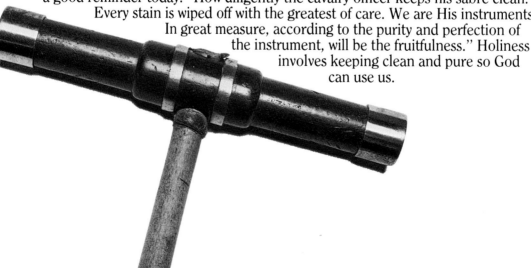

The shipbuilder lives to build ships. This is his pursuit in life. The Christian's aim is to magnify Christ.

The overriding concern of Paul's life was knowing and following Jesus Christ. He was not concerned with himself, his reputation, whether he was free or in prison, or even whether he lived or died. He awakened to each new day with one consuming desire . . . that Christ might be magnified through his life.

This supreme concern focused all his faculties and activities (his energy, relationships, prayers, interests, and writings) in one direction: the magnification of Christ.

In the light of Paul's example, Bishop Moule, in his exposition on Philippians, suggests that we ask ourselves some "very old-fashioned" questions:

"Is my life so lived and my work so done in contact with Him that through Him and not merely through myself my fruit is found?

"Is His promised day the goal and longing of my heart as I submit myself to Him that He may perfect His work in me and watch over me that I may meet Him single-hearted and without offense at the end?

"Is He the pervading and supreme interest of my life?"

"Is He the inward power which colors my thoughts and gives direction and quality to my affections?"

We cannot answer such questions glibly, but we should prayerfully consider them, saying, "Search me, O God, and know my heart . . ." (Psalm 139:23).

"Let your light so shine before men, that they may see your good works, and glorify your Father which is in heaven" (Matthew 5:16).

All ships have a name—even weekend craft. Are you identified?

There were three classes of persons in the ancient world who were branded on their bodies . . . soldiers, slaves, and devotees. The latter were temple slaves, and their brands indicated the god to whom each one belonged.

Paul declared his body was branded with the owner's stamp of the Lord Jesus: "I bear in my body the brandmarks of Jesus' ownership" (Galatians 6:17 BERK). He was referring, of course, to the scars inflicted by beatings and abuses suffered in his ministry for Christ. He was saying, in part, that there should be no doubt in a Christian's mind about belonging to Christ.

But what about us twentieth century Christians? Is our identification with Christ evident to those around us? How should our identity be communicated?

Paul tells us, "We Christians have the unmistakable 'scent' of Christ, discernible alike to those who are being saved and to those who are heading for death" (2 Corinthians 2:15 PH).

One means of identification is *the silent witness of a godly life*. Such a witness is the result of a carefully cultivated walk with Christ.

Another means of identification is *flying a verbal flag*. We do this by taking advantage of God-given opportunities to unhesitatingly talk about our faith in Christ. Paul's example is a good one to follow: "And pray for me, that I may be granted the right words when I open my mouth, . . . Pray that I may speak of it boldly, as it is my duty to speak" (Ephesians 6:19-20 NEB).

The ship's mast, jutting majestically into the sky, transfers the wind's power from the sails to the hull and drives the ship on its course. But if the mast were not counter balanced, the ship would capsize in the lightest breeze. A full one-third of a ship's weight should be ballast. What keeps a Christian on course in the seas of life? A balance between the knowledge of and the application of God's word.

Paul wanted to see the Christians at Philippi grow in godliness. He wanted to prepare them for the day they would enter the Lord's presence . . . so they could do so unashamed.

Love was to be the growing point in their lives. And this love was to be characterized by knowledge and discernment.

Knowledge in the New Testament always refers to the ways and will of God . . . as revealed in his word. The study of God's word is, therefore, essential to spiritual growth. Without *study*, a Christian's personal growth will be stunted.

But accumulating knowledge does not always produce a growing love. It can produce pride! To avoid such problems Paul harnesses knowledge with discernment.

Discernment adds the necessary balance, for it guides and shapes our application of Scripture to daily living. Knowledge is not intended primarily to *teach* us something, but to *make* us something. Applying the word to our life develops Christian character. Without *application*, growth will be stunted.

"The ultimate aim of the Christian ministry, after all, is to produce the love which springs from a pure heart, a good conscience and a genuine faith" (1 Timothy 1:5 PH).

It takes a long time to build a ship. An inbred characteristic of a shipbuilder is patience. And it takes a long time for a Christian to grow from his new birth to maturity.

Did you know that patience is a biblical characteristic that did not exist in ancient Greek society? To the Greeks, patience was no virtue; instead, men who refused to tolerate insults and who went all out for vengeance were admired.

Patience produces self-restraint (see James 5:7-11). Solomon also speaks eloquently of patience: "He that is slow to anger is *better* than the mighty; and *he that ruleth his spirit* than he that taketh a city" (Proverbs 16:32).

In the world's eyes, what a person accomplishes is far more important than what he *is* as a person. But God's word holds up the prophets and Job as examples for us to emulate. Did they build great pyramids or establish powerful kingdoms? Not at all! None of their accomplishments are cited. What is emphasized is their character—they were men of patience.

The Scriptures also show us that God is patient because he is slow to anger. It is patience that delays his judgment on men. Peter tells, us, "Bear in mind that our Lord's patience means salvation" (2 Peter 3:15 NIV).

Few passages describe his understanding and patience toward us more vividly than Psalm 103:10-14: "He hath not dealt with us after our sins; nor rewarded us according to our iniquities. For as the heaven is high above the earth, so great is his mercy toward them that fear him. As far as the east is from the west, so far hath he removed our transgressions from us. Like as a father pitieth his children, so the Lord pitieth them that fear him. For he knoweth our frame; he remembereth that we are dust."

If God deals with us like this—with such understanding and patience—shouldn't we deal patiently with others?

The commissioned ship sets forth on its mission.

Just before he left this earth, Jesus commissioned his disciples to take the gospel to every nation. They were the disciples of their generation. *We are the disciples of our generation.*

The commission is to us as much as to them. "God was in Christ personally reconciling the world to himself . . . and has *commissioned us* with the message of reconciliation" (2 Corinthians 5:19 PH).

It will be *through us* that Jesus either evangelizes the world or is hindered in evangelizing the world.

When God wants the message of the cross delivered, he looks for a man or woman through whom he can act.

We are often reminded about God's limitless power, but how often do we think about the helplessness of God? Unless God can find a person to do his work, God's work will never be done.

The angel who appeared to Cornelius told him how to find Peter who would then explain the way of salvation. The angel identified the man (Peter), the town (Joppa), the house (Simon's), its location (by the sea), but not the gospel . . . because *God has ordained that men perform this task.*

"For everyone, as it says again—'everyone who invokes the name of the Lord will be saved.' How could they invoke one in whom they had no faith? And how could they have faith in one they had never heard of? And how hear without someone to spread the news?" (Romans 10:13-14 NEB).